# WHAT IF THERE WERE NO GRAY WOLVES?

A Book about the Temperate Forest Ecosystem

by Suzanne Slade

Illustrated by Carol Schwartz

GRAY WOLVES ARE THE KINGS of the temperate forest. They hunt and howl between the leafy trees. And they share their wooded home with all sorts of feathered and furry creatures, from the tiniest songbird to the biggest moose.

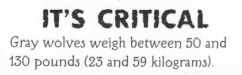

## IT'S CRITICAL

Gray wolves weigh between 50 and 130 pounds (23 and 59 kilograms).

**ALL LIVING THINGS** in the temperate forest ecosystem depend on each other for food. Plants and animals are connected to one another in a food chain. A gray wolf might dine on a deer for dinner. Deer graze on green plants. When many food chains connect, they form a food web.

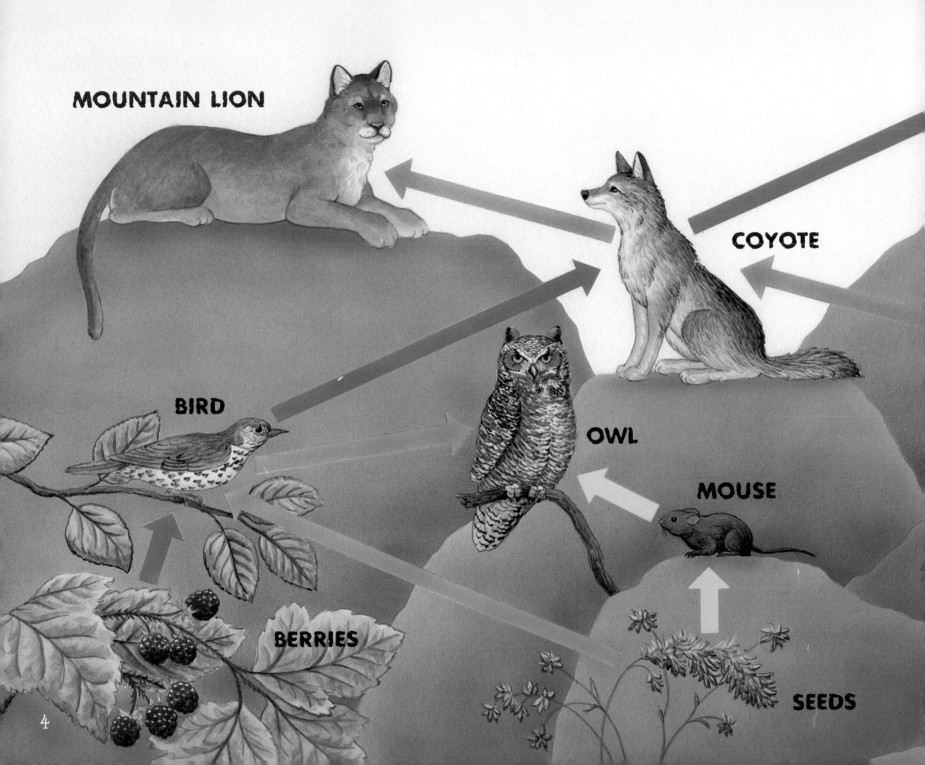

MOUNTAIN LION

COYOTE

BIRD

OWL

MOUSE

BERRIES

SEEDS

**GRAY WOLF**

## IT'S CRITICAL

Sometimes a plant or animal species is so important that without it many other species may become extinct. It's called a keystone species. Gray wolves are a keystone species. Keystone species help make sure an ecosystem has many types of life in it.

**ELK**

**DEER**

**RED FOX**

**SQUIRREL**

**GREEN PLANTS**

**NUTS**

5

GRAY WOLVES have an important job at the top of their food chain. They can eat up to 20 pounds (9 kg) of meat at one meal. A lone wolf may hunt for rabbits, beavers, and other small mammals. A pack of wolves will hunt bigger animals such as moose, elk, bison, and white-tailed deer.

## IT'S CRITICAL

Gray wolves are meat-eaters, or carnivores. They need meat to survive. Wolves use their keen sense of smell to hunt for their meals.

# IT'S CRITICAL

Today, states with large numbers of gray wolves may
choose to allow wolf hunting for short periods of time.

**GRAY WOLVES** don't need to fear other animals. But they do have to watch out for people. At one time, people had killed so many wolves that the wolves nearly disappeared. Then the U.S. government passed laws to protect wolves, and the animals' population began to grow. Today, hunters and ranchers wanting to protect their cattle are threats. So are people who destroy the wolves' homes to build new houses and businesses.

9

**WHAT WOULD HAPPEN** if gray wolves became extinct?

Without gray wolves, the animals they eat would begin to fill the forest. This would be especially true for larger prey, such as white-tailed deer. Deer have few predators besides wolves.

## IT'S CRITICAL

Mountain lions also hunt white-tailed deer. However, few mountain lions still remain in the forest. Hunters and people building new houses have destroyed the lions' homes.

**AS MORE AND MORE** white-tailed deer filled the forest, this leafy place would change.

Deer like to graze on leaves, crunchy twigs, nuts, berries, and plant buds. Before long, hungry white-tailed deer would eat nearly all ground-level plants.

## IT'S CRITICAL

Plants use sunlight, carbon dioxide, and water to make their own food. The food-making process is called photosynthesis.

13

**OTHER FOREST ANIMALS**, such as birds, squirrels, and moose, eat plants too. Mice and rabbits use plants for protection, hiding in thick bushes or beneath leaves. If white-tailed deer ate all the plants, these animals would either starve or become easy prey for meat-eaters.

# IT'S CRITICAL

When white-tailed deer can't find enough forest plants, they're often forced to cross busy roads to find food. Many deer cause vehicle accidents and are killed.

**SOON THE DEER THEMSELVES** would run out of food. They would disappear along with the smaller animals. Predators such as owls, coyotes, and foxes would face a food shortage of their own. Without a supply of meat, these animals couldn't survive.

## IT'S CRITICAL

Great gray owls make their homes in forest trees. About 90 percent of their meals come from small rodents, such as mice and gophers.

17

**WITHOUT GRAY WOLVES,** temperate forests would become quiet, empty places.

**NO BIRDS FILLING THE AIR WITH SONG.**

**NO SQUIRRELS SCAMPERING ACROSS THE FOREST FLOOR.**

NO RABBITS OR MICE
RUSTLING IN THE BUSHES.

What would happen if gray wolves became extinct?
**MORE THAN YOU MIGHT THINK!**

The loss of one animal, such as the mighty gray wolf, would have a big effect on our temperate forests.

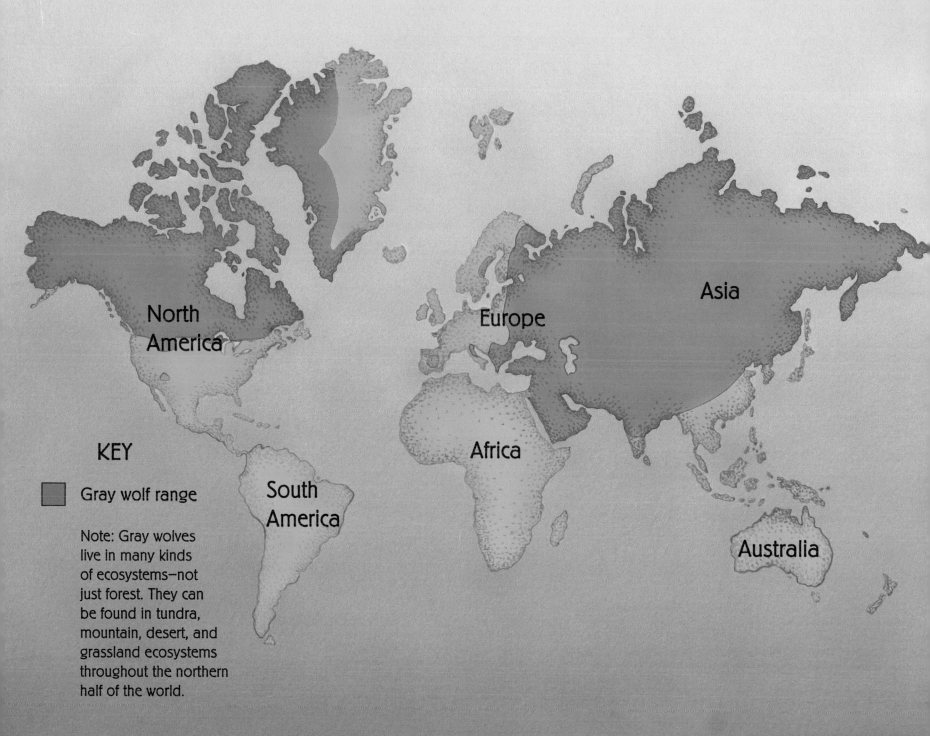

KEY

Gray wolf range

Note: Gray wolves live in many kinds of ecosystems—not just forest. They can be found in tundra, mountain, desert, and grassland ecosystems throughout the northern half of the world.

North America

Europe

Asia

Africa

South America

Australia

Today, people are working hard to protect forest ecosystems around the world. Wildlife workers are also closely watching gray wolves to make sure the food chains in our forests stay healthy and strong.

# TEMPERATE FOREST ANIMALS IN DANGER

The following animal populations are in danger of becoming extinct if nothing is done to protect them:

forest owlet
red wolf
grizzly bear
gray wolf
American burying beetle

American burying beetle

## HOW TO HELP KEEP OUR FORESTS HEALTHY

- When you visit a forest, be sure to leave it just as you found it. You can keep our forests clean by not littering. Some animals try to eat litter, which can poison them or cause them to choke.

- If you go camping in a forest, take extra care with campfires. Have an adult help you, and don't light fires unless the campground allows them. Light fires only in specially marked areas. Be sure to put out your fire with water before you leave the site.

- Help save trees by buying recycled paper products. Write on the blank side of used paper. Using less paper means more trees in our forests.

- Join a wildlife or nature group near you. Many groups offer special events to help protect our forests, such as cleanup days.

# Glossary

**carbon dioxide**—a gas that animals and people breathe out
**ecosystem**—a group of plants and animals living together, along with the place where they live
**extinct**—no longer living anywhere on Earth
**food chain**—a group of living things that are connected because each one eats the other
**food web**—many food chains connected together
**mammal**—a warm-blooded animal that feeds its young milk and has fur or hair
**predator**—an animal that hunts other animals for food
**prey**—an animal that is hunted by another animal for food
**species**—a group of plants or animals that has many things in common
**temperate**—mild; temperate forests have neither very hot nor very cold temperatures

# To Learn More

## More Books to Read

Brandenburg, Jim, and Judy. *Face to Face with Wolves.* Face to Face with Animals. Washington, D.C.: National Geographic, 2008.

Fleisher, Paul. *Forest Food Webs.* Early Bird Food Webs. Minneapolis: Lerner Publications Co., 2008.

Lundgren, Julie K. *Forest Fare: Studying Food Webs in the Forest.* Studying Food Webs. Vero Beach, Fla.: Rourke Pub., 2009.

## Internet Sites

FactHound offers a safe, fun way to find Internet sites related to this book.
All of the sites on FactHound have been researched by our staff.

Here's all you do:
Visit *www.facthound.com*
Type in this code: 9781404860209

# Index

## Look for all the books in the Food Chain Reactions series:

What If There Were No Bees? A Book about the Grassland Ecosystem

What If There Were No Gray Wolves? A Book about the Temperate Forest Ecosystem

What If There Were No Lemmings? A Book about the Tundra Ecosystem

What If There Were No Sea Otters? A Book about the Ocean Ecosystem

Special thanks to our advisers for their expertise:
Jess Edberg, Information Services Director
International Wolf Center, Ely, Minnesota

Terry Flaherty, PhD, Professor of English
Minnesota State University, Mankato

Picture Window Books
151 Good Counsel Drive
P.O. Box 669
Mankato, MN 56002-0669
877-845-8392
www.capstonepub.com

Editor: Jill Kalz
Designer: Lori Bye
Art Director: Nathan Gassman
Production Specialist: Jane Klenk
The illustrations in this book were created with traditional illustration, gouache, airbrush, and digitally.

Library of Congress Cataloging-in-Publication Data
Slade, Suzanne.
   What if there were no gray wolves! : a book about the temperate forest ecosystem / by Suzanne Slade ; illustrated by Carol Schwartz.
       p. cm. – (Food chain reactions)
   Includes bibliographical references and index.
   ISBN 978-1-4048-6020-9 (library binding)
   ISBN 978-1-4048-6395-8 (paperback)
   1. Forest ecology–North America. 2. Gray wolf–Habitat–Juvenile literature. I. Schwartz, Carol, 1954– ill. II. Title.
   QH541.5.F6S63 2011
   577.3097–dc22
                                        2010009877

Printed in the United States of America in North Mankato, Minnesota.
082011      006312R